BUSINE$$ OFFENSE

How to Win with People, Process, and Technology

PLAYBOOK

Brian Benton

WESTBOW
PRESS®
A DIVISION OF THOMAS NELSON
& ZONDERVAN

Scripture quotations marked (NIV) are taken from the Holy Bible, New International Version®, NIV®. Copyright © 1973, 1978, 1984 by Biblica, Inc.™ Used by permission of Zondervan. All rights reserved worldwide.

Scripture marked (NASB) taken from the New American Standard Bible®, Copyright© 1960, 1962, 1963, 1986, 1971, 1972, 1973, 1975, 1977, 1995 by The Lockman Foundation. Used by permission.

Scripture quotations marked (ESV) are from The Holy Bible, English Standard Version® (ESV®), copyright © 2001 by Crossway, a publishing ministry of Good News Publishers. Used by permission. All rights reserved.

WestBow Press books may be ordered through booksellers or by contacting:

WestBow Press
A Division of Thomas Nelson & Zondervan
1663 Liberty Drive
Bloomington, IN 47403
www.westbowpress.com
1 (866) 928-1240

ISBN: 978-1-9736-2114-0 (sc)
ISBN: 978-1-9736-2115-7 (e)

Library of Congress Control Number: 2018902582

Print information available on the last page.

WestBow Press rev. date: 10/23/2018

BUSINE$$
OFFENSE

How to Win with People, Process, and Technology

NAME:_____

ADDRESS:_____

PHONE:_____

EMAIL:_____

**BUSINE$$
OFFENSE**

How to Win with People, Process, and Technology

THE PLAYBOOK TO HELP YOU WIN WITH PEOPLE, PROCESS, AND TECHNOLOGY

VISIT BUSINESSOFFENSE.COM FOR TOOLS AND RESOURCES AS WELL AS INFORMATION ON TRAINING AND COACHING PROGRAMS.

CONTENTS

BUSINESS OFFENSE FUNDAMENTALS

THE FUNDAMENTALS OF THE BUSINESS OFFENSE ARE

PURPOSE, VALUES, STRATEGY, AND VISION.

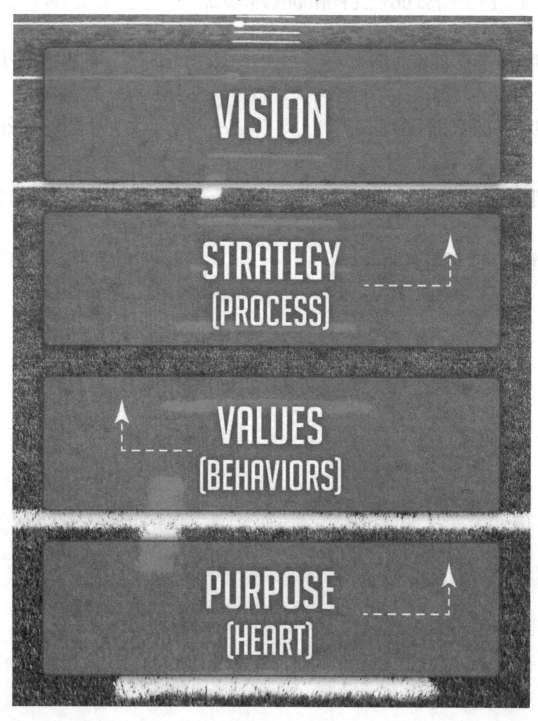

BUSINESS OFFENSE GAME PLAN

THE PURPOSE OF THE GAME PLAN WORKSHEET IS TO HELP EVERY EMPLOYEE VISUALLY SEE HOW THEY CONNECT WITH THE PURPOSE, VALUES, VISION, AND STRATEGY OF THE BUSINESS BY ALLOWING EVERY EMPLOYEE TO CREATE A QUARTERLY GAME PLAN ALIGNED WITH THE OVERALL BUSINESS GAME PLAN.

BUSINESS OFFENSE PLAYBOOK – THE GAME PLAN

BUSINESS NAME:

PURPOSE	VALUES	VISION

SUPERPOWER

COMPANY GAME PLAN

LEAD GEN	SALES	SCALE

BUSINESS OFFENSE PLAYBOOK – THE GAME PLAN

MY QUARTERLY GAME PLAN

NAME:	ACCOUNTABILITY PARTNER:	DUE DATE:

TRAINING

LEAD GEN	SALES	SCALE

GAMIFY/REWARD

BUSINESS OFFENSE GAME PLAN ADJUSTMENTS

THE BUSINESS OFFENSE GAME PLAN MUST BE ADJUSTED EVERY QUARTER TO CONTINUE TO COMPETE IN THE FAST-PACED BUSINESS WORLD.

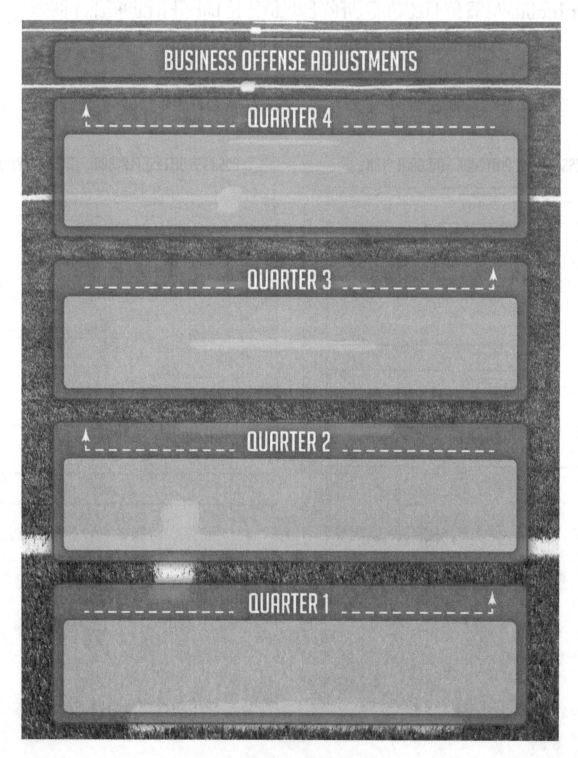

BUSINESS OFFENSE GAME PLAN ADJUSTMENTS WORKSHEET

THE BUSINESS OFFENSE GAME PLAN ADJUSTMENTS WORKSHEET
HELPS YOUR BUSINESS VISUALIZE THE MOST
IMPORTANT THINGS TO ADJUST EVERY QUARTER.

BUSINESS OFFENSE PLAYBOOK – GAME PLAN ADJUSTMENTS

WHAT ARE THE 3 TO 5 MOST IMPORTANT THINGS WE LEARNED ABOUT OUR EXECUTION IN THE PAST 90 DAYS?

WHAT ARE THE 20% OF ACTIVITIES THAT WILL GENERATE 80% OF THE RESULTS IN THE NEXT 90 DAYS?

HOW CAN WE MAKE WORK FUN AND REWARD EMPLOYEES FOR PERFORMANCE IN THE NEXT 90 DAYS?

DEVELOP YOUR MY COMPANY GAME PLAN

- COMPLETE THE TOP AND MIDDLE SECTION WITH BUSINESS NAME, PURPOSE, VALUES, VISION, AND SUPERPOWER.

- COMPLETE THE BOTTOM SECTION WITH THE COMPANY WIDE ANNUAL GOALS/TARGETS FOR: LEAD GEN, SALES, AND SCALE.

DEVELOP YOUR MY QUARTERLY GAME PLAN

- NAME: INCLUDE YOUR FIRST AND LAST NAME TO PERSONALIZE YOUR GAME PLAN.

- ACCOUNTABILITY: INCLUDE THE NAME OF THE PERSON THAT WILL ENCOURAGE YOU TO EXECUTE YOUR QUARTERLY GAME PLAN.

- DUE DATE: INCLUDE THE DATE AT THE END OF THE QUARTER.

- TRAINING: LIST THE TRAINING YOU WILL COMPLETE FOR THE QUARTER.

- LEAD GEN: LIST YOUR LEAD GENERATION TARGETS FOR THE QUARTER.

- SALES: LIST YOUR REVENUE TARGETS TO CONVERT LEADS FOR THE QUARTER.

- SCALE: LIST THE MOST IMPORTANT ACTIVITIES YOU WILL PERFORM TO HELP YOUR BUSINESS SCALE DURING THE QUARTER.

- COMPLETE THE GAMIFY/REWARD SECTION OF THE BUSINESS OFFENSE GAME PLAN WITH THE INCENTIVES YOU WILL RECEIVE AFTER YOU EXECUTE YOUR QUARTERLY GAME PLAN.

IMPORTANT NOTE: WE INCLUDED TWO COPIES OF THE GAME PLAN TO USE THE FIRST WORKSHEET AS THE DRAFT AND THE SECOND WORKSHEET AS THE PRODUCTION WORKSHEET.

PRACTICE DAILY ON THE "SHIPS"

- ## VERTICAL RELATIONSHIP:

  - HOW WILL I BUILD MY RELATIONSHIP WITH GOD TODAY?

- ## HORIZONTAL RELATIONSHIPS:

  - WHO DO I NEED TO FOCUS ON BUILDING A RELATIONSHIP WITH TODAY?

- ## LEADERSHIP:

  - HOW WILL I DEVELOP MY LEADERSHIP SKILLS TODAY?

  - WHO CAN I HELP DEVELOP THEIR LEADERSHIP SKILLS TODAY?

PRACTICE DAILY ON LEAD GEN, SALES, AND SCALE

- ## LEAD GEN:

  - WHAT DO I NEED TO FOCUS ON TODAY TO WORK TOWARDS ACHIEVING MY LEAD GEN TARGET?

- ## SALES:

  - WHAT DO I NEED TO FOCUS ON TODAY TO WORK TOWARDS ACHIEVING MY SALES TARGET?

- ## SCALE:

  - WHAT DO I NEED TO FOCUS ON TODAY TO WORK TOWARDS ACHIEVING MY SCALE TARGET?

DEVELOP YOUR SCORECARD

YOU CAN HAVE THE GREATEST STRATEGY OR GAME PLAN ON PLANET EARTH BUT IF YOU DON'T SCORE THE STRATEGY YOU WON'T KNOW IF YOU ARE IMPROVING. THE BIBLE SAYS IT THIS WAY *KNOW WELL THE CONDITION OF YOUR FLOCKS, AND PAY ATTENTION TO YOUR HERDS.* (PROVERBS 27:23 NASB) YOU HAVE TO PAY ATTENTION TO THE PERFORMANCE OF YOUR STRATEGY BY THE NUMBERS. THE SAYING RUN THE BUSINESS BY THE NUMBERS APPLIES TO ALL BUSINESSES REGARDLESS OF SIZE. THE SCORECARD IS A SIMPLE WAY TO TRACK THE KEY PERFORMANCE INDICATORS OF LEAD GEN, SALES, AND SCALE.

ADJUST YOUR GAME PLAN

THE PURPOSE OF YOUR QUARTERLY GAME PLAN ADJUSTMENT IS TO INCLUDE THE RIGHT PEOPLE TO ASK THE RIGHT QUESTIONS TO BUILD AN ACTION PLAN TO EXECUTE THE NEXT QUARTER. THE "RIGHT PEOPLE" CAN BE ANYONE IN THE ORGANIZATION OR OUTSIDE THE ORGANIZATION YOU TRUST TO PROVIDE VALUABLE FEEDBACK AND CAN HELP YOU MOVE THE BUSINESS FORWARD. YOU WANT TO ASK THE "RIGHT QUESTIONS" TO NARROW THE FOCUS OF THE ACTION PLAN. THE ACTION PLAN SHOULD FOCUS ON GENERATING LEADS, SALES, AND SCALE WHILE MAKING THE WORK FUN AND EXCITING. THE BEST PRACTICE IS TO BLOCK OFF ONE DAY PER QUARTER SOMEWHERE WITH NO DISTRACTIONS AND GOOD FOOD TO ASK THE RIGHT QUESTIONS.

- COMPLETE THE TOP SECTION BY ASKING: WHAT ARE THE 3 TO 5 MOST IMPORTANT THINGS WE LEARNED ABOUT OUR STRATEGY IN THE LAST 90 DAYS?

- COMPLETE THE MIDDLE SECTION BY ASKING: WHAT 20% OF ACTIVITIES WILL PRODUCE 80% OF THE RESULTS IN THE NEXT 90 DAYS?

- COMPLETE THE BOTTOM SECTION BY ASKING: HOW CAN WE MAKE EXECUTING OUR STRATEGY FUN WITH PRIZES, GIFTS, PARTIES, AND INCENTIVES TO BUILD STRONG TEAMS AND PROMOTE COOPERATION?

NOTES

BUSINESS OFFENSE PLAYBOOK – THE GAME PLAN

BUSINESS NAME:

PURPOSE

VALUES

VISION

SUPERPOWER

COMPANY GAME PLAN

LEAD GEN

SALES

SCALE

BUSINESS OFFENSE PLAYBOOK – THE GAME PLAN

MY QUARTERLY GAME PLAN

NAME:

ACCOUNTABILITY PARTNER:

DUE DATE:

TRAINING

LEAD GEN

SALES

SCALE

GAMIFY/REWARD

BUSINESS OFFENSE PLAYBOOK – THE GAME PLAN

BUSINESS NAME:

PURPOSE

VALUES

VISION

SUPERPOWER

COMPANY GAME PLAN

LEAD GEN

SALES

SCALE

BUSINESS OFFENSE PLAYBOOK – THE GAME PLAN

MY QUARTERLY GAME PLAN

NAME:

ACCOUNTABILITY PARTNER:

DUE DATE:

TRAINING

LEAD GEN

SALES

SCALE

GAMIFY/REWARD

PRACTICE DAILY ON THE "SHIPS"

VERTICAL RELATIONSHIP

HORIZONTAL RELATIONSHIPS

LEADERSHIP

PRACTICE DAILY ON LEAD GEN, SALES, AND SCALE

LEAD GEN

SALES

SCALE

PRACTICE DAILY ON THE "SHIPS"

VERTICAL RELATIONSHIP

HORIZONTAL RELATIONSHIPS

LEADERSHIP

PRACTICE DAILY ON LEAD GEN, SALES, AND SCALE

LEAD GEN

SALES

SCALE

PRACTICE DAILY ON THE "SHIPS"

VERTICAL RELATIONSHIP

HORIZONTAL RELATIONSHIPS

LEADERSHIP

PRACTICE DAILY ON LEAD GEN, SALES, AND SCALE

LEAD GEN

SALES

SCALE

PRACTICE DAILY ON THE "SHIPS"

VERTICAL RELATIONSHIP

HORIZONTAL RELATIONSHIPS

LEADERSHIP

PRACTICE DAILY ON LEAD GEN, SALES, AND SCALE

LEAD GEN

SALES

SCALE

PRACTICE DAILY ON THE "SHIPS"

VERTICAL RELATIONSHIP

HORIZONTAL RELATIONSHIPS

LEADERSHIP

PRACTICE DAILY ON LEAD GEN, SALES, AND SCALE

LEAD GEN

SALES

SCALE

PRACTICE DAILY ON THE "SHIPS"

VERTICAL RELATIONSHIP

HORIZONTAL RELATIONSHIPS

LEADERSHIP

PRACTICE DAILY ON LEAD GEN, SALES, AND SCALE

LEAD GEN

SALES

SCALE

PRACTICE DAILY ON THE "SHIPS"

VERTICAL RELATIONSHIP

HORIZONTAL RELATIONSHIPS

LEADERSHIP

PRACTICE DAILY ON LEAD GEN, SALES, AND SCALE

LEAD GEN

SALES

SCALE

PRACTICE DAILY ON THE "SHIPS"

VERTICAL RELATIONSHIP

HORIZONTAL RELATIONSHIPS

LEADERSHIP

PRACTICE DAILY ON LEAD GEN, SALES, AND SCALE

LEAD GEN

SALES

SCALE

PRACTICE DAILY ON THE "SHIPS"

VERTICAL RELATIONSHIP

HORIZONTAL RELATIONSHIPS

LEADERSHIP

PRACTICE DAILY ON LEAD GEN, SALES, AND SCALE

LEAD GEN

SALES

SCALE

PRACTICE DAILY ON THE "SHIPS"

VERTICAL RELATIONSHIP

HORIZONTAL RELATIONSHIPS

LEADERSHIP

PRACTICE DAILY ON LEAD GEN, SALES, AND SCALE

LEAD GEN

SALES

SCALE

PRACTICE DAILY ON THE "SHIPS"

VERTICAL RELATIONSHIP

HORIZONTAL RELATIONSHIPS

LEADERSHIP

PRACTICE DAILY ON LEAD GEN, SALES, AND SCALE

LEAD GEN

SALES

SCALE

PRACTICE DAILY ON THE "SHIPS"

VERTICAL RELATIONSHIP

HORIZONTAL RELATIONSHIPS

LEADERSHIP

PRACTICE DAILY ON LEAD GEN, SALES, AND SCALE

LEAD GEN

SALES

SCALE

PRACTICE DAILY ON THE "SHIPS"

VERTICAL RELATIONSHIP

HORIZONTAL RELATIONSHIPS

LEADERSHIP

PRACTICE DAILY ON LEAD GEN, SALES, AND SCALE

LEAD GEN

SALES

SCALE

PRACTICE DAILY ON THE "SHIPS"

VERTICAL RELATIONSHIP

HORIZONTAL RELATIONSHIPS

LEADERSHIP

PRACTICE DAILY ON LEAD GEN, SALES, AND SCALE

LEAD GEN

SALES

SCALE

PRACTICE DAILY ON THE "SHIPS"

VERTICAL RELATIONSHIP

HORIZONTAL RELATIONSHIPS

LEADERSHIP

PRACTICE DAILY ON LEAD GEN, SALES, AND SCALE

LEAD GEN

SALES

SCALE

PRACTICE DAILY ON THE "SHIPS"

VERTICAL RELATIONSHIP

HORIZONTAL RELATIONSHIPS

LEADERSHIP

PRACTICE DAILY ON LEAD GEN, SALES, AND SCALE

LEAD GEN

SALES

SCALE

PRACTICE DAILY ON THE "SHIPS"

VERTICAL RELATIONSHIP

HORIZONTAL RELATIONSHIPS

LEADERSHIP

PRACTICE DAILY ON LEAD GEN, SALES, AND SCALE

LEAD GEN

SALES

SCALE

PRACTICE DAILY ON THE "SHIPS"

VERTICAL RELATIONSHIP

HORIZONTAL RELATIONSHIPS

LEADERSHIP

PRACTICE DAILY ON LEAD GEN, SALES, AND SCALE

LEAD GEN

SALES

SCALE

PRACTICE DAILY ON THE "SHIPS"

VERTICAL RELATIONSHIP

HORIZONTAL RELATIONSHIPS

LEADERSHIP

PRACTICE DAILY ON LEAD GEN, SALES, AND SCALE

LEAD GEN

SALES

SCALE

PRACTICE DAILY ON THE "SHIPS"

VERTICAL RELATIONSHIP

HORIZONTAL RELATIONSHIPS

LEADERSHIP

PRACTICE DAILY ON LEAD GEN, SALES, AND SCALE

LEAD GEN

SALES

SCALE

PRACTICE DAILY ON THE "SHIPS"

VERTICAL RELATIONSHIP

HORIZONTAL RELATIONSHIPS

LEADERSHIP

PRACTICE DAILY ON LEAD GEN, SALES, AND SCALE

LEAD GEN

SALES

SCALE

PRACTICE DAILY ON THE "SHIPS"

VERTICAL RELATIONSHIP

HORIZONTAL RELATIONSHIPS

LEADERSHIP

PRACTICE DAILY ON LEAD GEN, SALES, AND SCALE

LEAD GEN

SALES

SCALE

PRACTICE DAILY ON THE "SHIPS"

<u>VERTICAL RELATIONSHIP</u>

<u>HORIZONTAL RELATIONSHIPS</u>

<u>LEADERSHIP</u>

PRACTICE DAILY ON LEAD GEN, SALES, AND SCALE

LEAD GEN

SALES

SCALE

PRACTICE DAILY ON THE "SHIPS"

VERTICAL RELATIONSHIP

HORIZONTAL RELATIONSHIPS

LEADERSHIP

PRACTICE DAILY ON LEAD GEN, SALES, AND SCALE

LEAD GEN

SALES

SCALE

PRACTICE DAILY ON THE "SHIPS"

VERTICAL RELATIONSHIP

HORIZONTAL RELATIONSHIPS

LEADERSHIP

PRACTICE DAILY ON LEAD GEN, SALES, AND SCALE

LEAD GEN

SALES

SCALE

PRACTICE DAILY ON THE "SHIPS"

VERTICAL RELATIONSHIP

HORIZONTAL RELATIONSHIPS

LEADERSHIP

PRACTICE DAILY ON LEAD GEN, SALES, AND SCALE

LEAD GEN

SALES

SCALE

PRACTICE DAILY ON THE "SHIPS"

VERTICAL RELATIONSHIP

HORIZONTAL RELATIONSHIPS

LEADERSHIP

PRACTICE DAILY ON LEAD GEN, SALES, AND SCALE

LEAD GEN

SALES

SCALE

PRACTICE DAILY ON THE "SHIPS"

VERTICAL RELATIONSHIP

HORIZONTAL RELATIONSHIPS

LEADERSHIP

PRACTICE DAILY ON LEAD GEN, SALES, AND SCALE

LEAD GEN

SALES

SCALE

PRACTICE DAILY ON THE "SHIPS"

VERTICAL RELATIONSHIP

HORIZONTAL RELATIONSHIPS

LEADERSHIP

PRACTICE DAILY ON LEAD GEN, SALES, AND SCALE

LEAD GEN

SALES

SCALE

PRACTICE DAILY ON THE "SHIPS"

VERTICAL RELATIONSHIP

HORIZONTAL RELATIONSHIPS

LEADERSHIP

PRACTICE DAILY ON LEAD GEN, SALES, AND SCALE

LEAD GEN

SALES

SCALE

PRACTICE DAILY ON THE "SHIPS"

VERTICAL RELATIONSHIP

HORIZONTAL RELATIONSHIPS

LEADERSHIP

PRACTICE DAILY ON LEAD GEN, SALES, AND SCALE

LEAD GEN

SALES

SCALE

PRACTICE DAILY ON THE "SHIPS"

VERTICAL RELATIONSHIP

HORIZONTAL RELATIONSHIPS

LEADERSHIP

PRACTICE DAILY ON LEAD GEN, SALES, AND SCALE

LEAD GEN

SALES

SCALE

PRACTICE DAILY ON THE "SHIPS"

VERTICAL RELATIONSHIP

HORIZONTAL RELATIONSHIPS

LEADERSHIP

PRACTICE DAILY ON LEAD GEN, SALES, AND SCALE

LEAD GEN

SALES

SCALE

PRACTICE DAILY ON THE "SHIPS"

VERTICAL RELATIONSHIP

HORIZONTAL RELATIONSHIPS

LEADERSHIP

PRACTICE DAILY ON LEAD GEN, SALES, AND SCALE

LEAD GEN

SALES

SCALE

PRACTICE DAILY ON THE "SHIPS"

VERTICAL RELATIONSHIP

HORIZONTAL RELATIONSHIPS

LEADERSHIP

PRACTICE DAILY ON LEAD GEN, SALES, AND SCALE

LEAD GEN

SALES

SCALE

PRACTICE DAILY ON THE "SHIPS"

VERTICAL RELATIONSHIP

HORIZONTAL RELATIONSHIPS

LEADERSHIP

PRACTICE DAILY ON LEAD GEN, SALES, AND SCALE

LEAD GEN

SALES

SCALE

PRACTICE DAILY ON THE "SHIPS"

VERTICAL RELATIONSHIP

HORIZONTAL RELATIONSHIPS

LEADERSHIP

PRACTICE DAILY ON LEAD GEN, SALES, AND SCALE

LEAD GEN

SALES

SCALE

PRACTICE DAILY ON THE "SHIPS"

<u>VERTICAL RELATIONSHIP</u>

<u>HORIZONTAL RELATIONSHIPS</u>

<u>LEADERSHIP</u>

PRACTICE DAILY ON LEAD GEN, SALES, AND SCALE

LEAD GEN

SALES

SCALE

PRACTICE DAILY ON THE "SHIPS"

<u>VERTICAL RELATIONSHIP</u>

<u>HORIZONTAL RELATIONSHIPS</u>

<u>LEADERSHIP</u>

PRACTICE DAILY ON LEAD GEN, SALES, AND SCALE

LEAD GEN

SALES

SCALE

PRACTICE DAILY ON THE "SHIPS"

VERTICAL RELATIONSHIP

HORIZONTAL RELATIONSHIPS

LEADERSHIP

PRACTICE DAILY ON LEAD GEN, SALES, AND SCALE

LEAD GEN

SALES

SCALE

PRACTICE DAILY ON THE "SHIPS"

VERTICAL RELATIONSHIP

HORIZONTAL RELATIONSHIPS

LEADERSHIP

PRACTICE DAILY ON LEAD GEN, SALES, AND SCALE

LEAD GEN

SALES

SCALE

PRACTICE DAILY ON THE "SHIPS"

VERTICAL RELATIONSHIP

HORIZONTAL RELATIONSHIPS

LEADERSHIP

PRACTICE DAILY ON LEAD GEN, SALES, AND SCALE

LEAD GEN

SALES

SCALE

PRACTICE DAILY ON THE "SHIPS"

VERTICAL RELATIONSHIP

HORIZONTAL RELATIONSHIPS

LEADERSHIP

PRACTICE DAILY ON LEAD GEN, SALES, AND SCALE

LEAD GEN

SALES

SCALE

PRACTICE DAILY ON THE "SHIPS"

VERTICAL RELATIONSHIP

HORIZONTAL RELATIONSHIPS

LEADERSHIP

PRACTICE DAILY ON LEAD GEN, SALES, AND SCALE

LEAD GEN

SALES

SCALE

PRACTICE DAILY ON THE "SHIPS"

VERTICAL RELATIONSHIP

HORIZONTAL RELATIONSHIPS

LEADERSHIP

PRACTICE DAILY ON LEAD GEN, SALES, AND SCALE

LEAD GEN

SALES

SCALE

PRACTICE DAILY ON THE "SHIPS"

VERTICAL RELATIONSHIP

HORIZONTAL RELATIONSHIPS

LEADERSHIP

PRACTICE DAILY ON LEAD GEN, SALES, AND SCALE

LEAD GEN

SALES

SCALE

PRACTICE DAILY ON THE "SHIPS"

VERTICAL RELATIONSHIP

HORIZONTAL RELATIONSHIPS

LEADERSHIP

PRACTICE DAILY ON LEAD GEN, SALES, AND SCALE

LEAD GEN

SALES

SCALE

PRACTICE DAILY ON THE "SHIPS"

VERTICAL RELATIONSHIP

HORIZONTAL RELATIONSHIPS

LEADERSHIP

PRACTICE DAILY ON LEAD GEN, SALES, AND SCALE

LEAD GEN

SALES

SCALE

PRACTICE DAILY ON THE "SHIPS"

VERTICAL RELATIONSHIP

HORIZONTAL RELATIONSHIPS

LEADERSHIP

PRACTICE DAILY ON LEAD GEN, SALES, AND SCALE

LEAD GEN

SALES

SCALE

PRACTICE DAILY ON THE "SHIPS"

VERTICAL RELATIONSHIP

HORIZONTAL RELATIONSHIPS

LEADERSHIP

PRACTICE DAILY ON LEAD GEN, SALES, AND SCALE

LEAD GEN

SALES

SCALE

PRACTICE DAILY ON THE "SHIPS"

VERTICAL RELATIONSHIP

HORIZONTAL RELATIONSHIPS

LEADERSHIP

PRACTICE DAILY ON LEAD GEN, SALES, AND SCALE

LEAD GEN

SALES

SCALE

PRACTICE DAILY ON THE "SHIPS"

VERTICAL RELATIONSHIP

HORIZONTAL RELATIONSHIPS

LEADERSHIP

PRACTICE DAILY ON LEAD GEN, SALES, AND SCALE

LEAD GEN

SALES

SCALE

PRACTICE DAILY ON THE "SHIPS"

<u>VERTICAL RELATIONSHIP</u>

<u>HORIZONTAL RELATIONSHIPS</u>

<u>LEADERSHIP</u>

PRACTICE DAILY ON LEAD GEN, SALES, AND SCALE

LEAD GEN

SALES

SCALE

PRACTICE DAILY ON THE "SHIPS"

VERTICAL RELATIONSHIP

HORIZONTAL RELATIONSHIPS

LEADERSHIP

PRACTICE DAILY ON LEAD GEN, SALES, AND SCALE

LEAD GEN

SALES

SCALE

PRACTICE DAILY ON THE "SHIPS"

VERTICAL RELATIONSHIP

HORIZONTAL RELATIONSHIPS

LEADERSHIP

PRACTICE DAILY ON LEAD GEN, SALES, AND SCALE

LEAD GEN

SALES

SCALE

PRACTICE DAILY ON THE "SHIPS"

VERTICAL RELATIONSHIP

HORIZONTAL RELATIONSHIPS

LEADERSHIP

PRACTICE DAILY ON LEAD GEN, SALES, AND SCALE

LEAD GEN

SALES

SCALE

PRACTICE DAILY ON THE "SHIPS"

VERTICAL RELATIONSHIP

HORIZONTAL RELATIONSHIPS

LEADERSHIP

PRACTICE DAILY ON LEAD GEN, SALES, AND SCALE

LEAD GEN

SALES

SCALE

PRACTICE DAILY ON THE "SHIPS"

VERTICAL RELATIONSHIP

HORIZONTAL RELATIONSHIPS

LEADERSHIP

PRACTICE DAILY ON LEAD GEN, SALES, AND SCALE

LEAD GEN

SALES

SCALE

PRACTICE DAILY ON THE "SHIPS"

VERTICAL RELATIONSHIP

HORIZONTAL RELATIONSHIPS

LEADERSHIP

PRACTICE DAILY ON LEAD GEN, SALES, AND SCALE

LEAD GEN

SALES

SCALE

PRACTICE DAILY ON THE "SHIPS"

VERTICAL RELATIONSHIP

HORIZONTAL RELATIONSHIPS

LEADERSHIP

PRACTICE DAILY ON LEAD GEN, SALES, AND SCALE

LEAD GEN

SALES

SCALE

PRACTICE DAILY ON THE "SHIPS"

VERTICAL RELATIONSHIP

HORIZONTAL RELATIONSHIPS

LEADERSHIP

PRACTICE DAILY ON LEAD GEN, SALES, AND SCALE

LEAD GEN

SALES

SCALE

PRACTICE DAILY ON THE "SHIPS"

VERTICAL RELATIONSHIP

HORIZONTAL RELATIONSHIPS

LEADERSHIP

PRACTICE DAILY ON LEAD GEN, SALES, AND SCALE

LEAD GEN

SALES

SCALE

PRACTICE DAILY ON THE "SHIPS"

VERTICAL RELATIONSHIP

HORIZONTAL RELATIONSHIPS

LEADERSHIP

PRACTICE DAILY ON LEAD GEN, SALES, AND SCALE

LEAD GEN

SALES

SCALE

PRACTICE DAILY ON THE "SHIPS"

VERTICAL RELATIONSHIP

HORIZONTAL RELATIONSHIPS

LEADERSHIP

PRACTICE DAILY ON LEAD GEN, SALES, AND SCALE

LEAD GEN

SALES

SCALE

PRACTICE DAILY ON THE "SHIPS"

VERTICAL RELATIONSHIP

HORIZONTAL RELATIONSHIPS

LEADERSHIP

PRACTICE DAILY ON LEAD GEN, SALES, AND SCALE

LEAD GEN

SALES

SCALE

PRACTICE DAILY ON THE "SHIPS"

VERTICAL RELATIONSHIP

HORIZONTAL RELATIONSHIPS

LEADERSHIP

PRACTICE DAILY ON LEAD GEN, SALES, AND SCALE

LEAD GEN

SALES

SCALE

PRACTICE DAILY ON THE "SHIPS"

VERTICAL RELATIONSHIP

HORIZONTAL RELATIONSHIPS

LEADERSHIP

PRACTICE DAILY ON LEAD GEN, SALES, AND SCALE

LEAD GEN

SALES

SCALE

PRACTICE DAILY ON THE "SHIPS"

VERTICAL RELATIONSHIP

HORIZONTAL RELATIONSHIPS

LEADERSHIP

PRACTICE DAILY ON LEAD GEN, SALES, AND SCALE

LEAD GEN

SALES

SCALE

PRACTICE DAILY ON THE "SHIPS"

VERTICAL RELATIONSHIP

HORIZONTAL RELATIONSHIPS

LEADERSHIP

PRACTICE DAILY ON LEAD GEN, SALES, AND SCALE

LEAD GEN

SALES

SCALE

PRACTICE DAILY ON THE "SHIPS"

VERTICAL RELATIONSHIP

HORIZONTAL RELATIONSHIPS

LEADERSHIP

PRACTICE DAILY ON LEAD GEN, SALES, AND SCALE

LEAD GEN

SALES

SCALE

PRACTICE DAILY ON THE "SHIPS"

VERTICAL RELATIONSHIP

HORIZONTAL RELATIONSHIPS

LEADERSHIP

PRACTICE DAILY ON LEAD GEN, SALES, AND SCALE

LEAD GEN

SALES

SCALE

PRACTICE DAILY ON THE "SHIPS"

VERTICAL RELATIONSHIP

HORIZONTAL RELATIONSHIPS

LEADERSHIP

PRACTICE DAILY ON LEAD GEN, SALES, AND SCALE

LEAD GEN

SALES

SCALE

PRACTICE DAILY ON THE "SHIPS"

<u>VERTICAL RELATIONSHIP</u>

<u>HORIZONTAL RELATIONSHIPS</u>

<u>LEADERSHIP</u>

PRACTICE DAILY ON LEAD GEN, SALES, AND SCALE

LEAD GEN

SALES

SCALE

PRACTICE DAILY ON THE "SHIPS"

VERTICAL RELATIONSHIP

HORIZONTAL RELATIONSHIPS

LEADERSHIP

PRACTICE DAILY ON LEAD GEN, SALES, AND SCALE

LEAD GEN

SALES

SCALE

PRACTICE DAILY ON THE "SHIPS"

VERTICAL RELATIONSHIP

HORIZONTAL RELATIONSHIPS

LEADERSHIP

PRACTICE DAILY ON LEAD GEN, SALES, AND SCALE

LEAD GEN

SALES

SCALE

PRACTICE DAILY ON THE "SHIPS"

VERTICAL RELATIONSHIP

HORIZONTAL RELATIONSHIPS

LEADERSHIP

PRACTICE DAILY ON LEAD GEN, SALES, AND SCALE

LEAD GEN

SALES

SCALE

PRACTICE DAILY ON THE "SHIPS"

VERTICAL RELATIONSHIP

HORIZONTAL RELATIONSHIPS

LEADERSHIP

PRACTICE DAILY ON LEAD GEN, SALES, AND SCALE

LEAD GEN

SALES

SCALE

PRACTICE DAILY ON THE "SHIPS"

VERTICAL RELATIONSHIP

HORIZONTAL RELATIONSHIPS

LEADERSHIP

PRACTICE DAILY ON LEAD GEN, SALES, AND SCALE

LEAD GEN

SALES

SCALE

PRACTICE DAILY ON THE "SHIPS"

VERTICAL RELATIONSHIP

HORIZONTAL RELATIONSHIPS

LEADERSHIP

PRACTICE DAILY ON LEAD GEN, SALES, AND SCALE

LEAD GEN

SALES

SCALE

PRACTICE DAILY ON THE "SHIPS"

VERTICAL RELATIONSHIP

HORIZONTAL RELATIONSHIPS

LEADERSHIP

PRACTICE DAILY ON LEAD GEN, SALES, AND SCALE

LEAD GEN

SALES

SCALE

PRACTICE DAILY ON THE "SHIPS"

VERTICAL RELATIONSHIP

HORIZONTAL RELATIONSHIPS

LEADERSHIP

PRACTICE DAILY ON LEAD GEN, SALES, AND SCALE

LEAD GEN

SALES

SCALE

PRACTICE DAILY ON THE "SHIPS"

VERTICAL RELATIONSHIP

.

HORIZONTAL RELATIONSHIPS

LEADERSHIP

PRACTICE DAILY ON LEAD GEN, SALES, AND SCALE

LEAD GEN

SALES

SCALE

PRACTICE DAILY ON THE "SHIPS"

VERTICAL RELATIONSHIP

HORIZONTAL RELATIONSHIPS

LEADERSHIP

PRACTICE DAILY ON LEAD GEN, SALES, AND SCALE

LEAD GEN

SALES

SCALE

PRACTICE DAILY ON THE "SHIPS"

VERTICAL RELATIONSHIP

HORIZONTAL RELATIONSHIPS

LEADERSHIP

PRACTICE DAILY ON LEAD GEN, SALES, AND SCALE

LEAD GEN

SALES

SCALE

PRACTICE DAILY ON THE "SHIPS"

VERTICAL RELATIONSHIP

HORIZONTAL RELATIONSHIPS

LEADERSHIP

PRACTICE DAILY ON LEAD GEN, SALES, AND SCALE

LEAD GEN

SALES

SCALE

PRACTICE DAILY ON THE "SHIPS"

VERTICAL RELATIONSHIP

HORIZONTAL RELATIONSHIPS

LEADERSHIP

PRACTICE DAILY ON LEAD GEN, SALES, AND SCALE

LEAD GEN

SALES

SCALE

PRACTICE DAILY ON THE "SHIPS"

VERTICAL RELATIONSHIP

HORIZONTAL RELATIONSHIPS

LEADERSHIP

PRACTICE DAILY ON LEAD GEN, SALES, AND SCALE

LEAD GEN

SALES

SCALE

PRACTICE DAILY ON THE "SHIPS"

VERTICAL RELATIONSHIP

HORIZONTAL RELATIONSHIPS

LEADERSHIP

PRACTICE DAILY ON LEAD GEN, SALES, AND SCALE

LEAD GEN

SALES

SCALE

PRACTICE DAILY ON THE "SHIPS"

VERTICAL RELATIONSHIP

HORIZONTAL RELATIONSHIPS

LEADERSHIP

PRACTICE DAILY ON LEAD GEN, SALES, AND SCALE

LEAD GEN

SALES

SCALE

PRACTICE DAILY ON THE "SHIPS"

VERTICAL RELATIONSHIP

HORIZONTAL RELATIONSHIPS

LEADERSHIP

PRACTICE DAILY ON LEAD GEN, SALES, AND SCALE

LEAD GEN

SALES

SCALE

PRACTICE DAILY ON THE "SHIPS"

<u>VERTICAL RELATIONSHIP</u>

<u>HORIZONTAL RELATIONSHIPS</u>

<u>LEADERSHIP</u>

PRACTICE DAILY ON LEAD GEN, SALES, AND SCALE

LEAD GEN

SALES

SCALE

BUSINESS OFFENSE PLAYBOOK – SCORECARD

KPI	TARGET	SCORE	REWARD

LEAD GEN

SALES

SCALE

BUSINESS OFFENSE PLAYBOOK – SCORECARD

KPI	TARGET	SCORE	REWARD
LEAD GEN			
SALES			
SCALE			

BUSINESS OFFENSE PLAYBOOK – GAME PLAN ADJUSTMENTS

WHAT ARE THE 3 TO 5 MOST IMPORTANT THINGS WE LEARNED ABOUT OUR EXECUTION IN THE PAST 90 DAYS?

WHAT ARE THE 20% OF ACTIVITIES THAT WILL GENERATE 80% OF THE RESULTS IN THE NEXT 90 DAYS?

HOW CAN WE MAKE WORK FUN AND REWARD EMPLOYEES FOR PERFORMANCE IN THE NEXT 90 DAYS?

BUSINESS OFFENSE PLAYBOOK – GAME PLAN ADJUSTMENTS

WHAT ARE THE 3 TO 5 MOST IMPORTANT THINGS WE LEARNED ABOUT OUR EXECUTION IN THE PAST 90 DAYS?

WHAT ARE THE 20% OF ACTIVITIES THAT WILL GENERATE 80% OF THE RESULTS IN THE NEXT 90 DAYS?

HOW CAN WE MAKE WORK FUN AND REWARD EMPLOYEES FOR PERFORMANCE IN THE NEXT 90 DAYS?

Printed in the United States
By Bookmasters